Braille
for a
Storm of Loss

poems
by William Ruddy

with a foreword by William Everson

oyez / 1978

Drawings by J. Ronald Eli, O.P., except:
Number 3, Fawn from Henri Breuil's *Four Hundred Centuries of Cave Art,*
translated by Mary E. Boyle, Montignac, Centre des Etudes et de
Documentation Prehistoriques, 1952, page 68, figures 23 & 24.
Number 6, Women and Child from E. O. James's *Prehistoric Religion:
A Study in Prehistoric Archaeology,* New York, Barnes & Noble, Inc., 1962,
p. 149.
Number 8, Snake from Alexander Marshack's "Exploring the Mind of
Ice Age Man," *National Geographic,* January 1975, Vol. 147, No. 1,
page 62.

Foreword

In estimating the merit of any emerging poet, one of the first imperatives is to specify the precise weight and cogency of his influences. Yet this easily degenerates into condescension. The critic finds himself smelling out the most elusive of the poet's sources in order to present to the reader his own credentials. Only after having demonstrated his professional competency in this way does he feel free to proceed to what he actually opines about the work.

There are, however, other ways to go. In the present case, we have a young cleric, a budding priest-poet who overcame the liabilities of his clerical image by mixing bravely in the street-people-and-student unrest of Berkeley during the Sixties, writing verse in the loose idiom of his American generation. Then, out of a need to deepen his sources, he opted for a course of study at the University of Madras on the east coast of India. There he made friends with a native family and was adopted among them as a son and brother. From one point of view, the inevitable happened—the immersion deepened his writing into consequentiality: verse became poetry. But from a more profound perspective what actually happened was not inevitable at all, it was nothing short of miraculous. Genius is not the issue of process but of grace.

I first knew Father Ruddy as Brother William, a student friar at the Dominican House of Studies, St. Albert's College in Oakland California, where I myself served as a lay brother. He showed me his verse and I sensed immediately a truly perceptive ear, but felt as well a lack of inevitability. In time Brother William was ordained and sent off to teach in the Pacific Northwest where, true to his instincts, he sought out the same strata of vital street people and denizens of the outlying communes he had affiliated with in Berkeley. These finally and effectively dispelled any pretense of clerical image by affectionately nicknaming him "Willie."

In 1969 I left the Dominican community and settled in Stinson Beach, a shoreside community north of San Francisco. Fr. Ruddy visited me once in 1970 and again in 1971, announcing that he was going to complete his studies in Madras. It then seemed to me one of the signs of the times: a young cleric going off to India to imbibe the Wisdom of the East.

Now, three years later, Fr. Ruddy has returned. He has told me of his ordeal with the demonic following his adoption into a family of natives, and has placed in my hands an impressive book of poems. Sequentially arranged under the aspect of the approach, apotheosis and aftermath of a cyclone, it is actually the scenario of a profoundly personal Dantesque journey into the inner world of nightmare. For, truly, something happened to him in India, and it was not the intellectual acquisition of the Wisdom of the East, but a shocking encounter with the preternatural world simmering beneath native Indian life. Such is his capacity for basic human affinity that in their midst he could not insulate himself from the forces that motivated them, but must somehow transmute those forces into his own sensibility.

His first recourse, it goes without saying, was the Christ of his sacred ministry, but beyond that was his pen, and in writing these poems he reached far back for lingual sources, desperately needed expressive strengths, which proved not to be his congenial American affinities, but something more germane to the crisis he was undergoing. In his Acknowledgments he speaks of three saving presences that rose to his rescue—Gerard Manley Hopkins, Edith Sitwell, and Dylan Thomas—all British. But the wonderful thing to watch is his instinct in play as he saves himself from the onslaught with which the primitive beliefs of India overwhelmed him. By recourse to three distinct levels of evolving British sensibility, he emerges in India with a medium that is perfect for American survival there, the kind of intuitive coherence that transmutes technique into slavivic opportunity.

This takes us back to the matter of influences. We see how under pressure three separate but kindred spirits—the pre-modernist Hopkins, the modernist Sitwell and the post-modernist Thomas—fuse together in his direction to meet the situation of one who needs the essence of each to survive what he must undergo. In the same way certain instrumental combinations in orchestral music reveal tonalities common to each but unsuspected there until struck together to reveal plangencies out of the exigence of aesthetic need. Thus for all three deceased poets Fr. Ruddy's realization throws a light of mutuality back on the vibration of their own practice, one of the chief pertinencies of derivation in art. I believe all three would be gratified to find their presences synthesized in this way, rescuing, by endowing with expression, a fellow spirit from the forces that threatened him.

In the following pages we see a remarkable fusion. Here, in the guise of an American poet, out of the mystery of the East and the English tongue, come both the Serpent and the Dove.

WILLIAM EVERSON
Kresge College
University of California at Santa Cruz

Acknowledgments

These poems attempt to offer shelter for helpless loss. If a spiderweb is damaged, there can be no repairing. The spider begins again, completely anew, having within its nature a regained instinct, still intact, as a sort of braille-knowledge of limits. Poetry also, through its driving force of verbal feeling, intensified into speech, renews the entire ground of Being, thereby bringing into breathless focus exactly what our blinded childhood fashioned us to speak. This objectification of heart-felt feeling is very close to me, because my own brother is blind, and I remember how the rest of us had to deepen down our voice from ordinary, sighted speech as a kind of accommodation. Of course, all that it takes is love.

The poems in this book are meant to be a sort of braille for the heart. Basing myself on the experiences that happened to me during a three-years stay in Madras, India, I attempt to confront the total, soundless void of possessed loss: a web broken by pure storm. Such a wholly interior reworking of poetic form cannot rely on mere stoic description of fact. Thus I have, in the tradition of Hopkins, Sitwell, and Dylan Thomas, fallen back upon special ecstatic rhythms, of a directly alliterative and syncopated kind, which allow at last the creative imagination itself to offer pure solace to loss somewhat in the same trance-like way in which Indian drum-chants give formal relief to the grief of a funeral procession.

Such a deeply patterned-out device, with its stress on words such as "dome" as a mirror for the Hindu chanting of OM, may seem at first cumbersome. I can only suggest that the reader gain back each poem's balance of form by simply reading it out loud with a syncopated emphasis on adjectives, leading into the direct beat on the final verb or noun. If language itself were ever to evolve a visual speech for the blind, I imagine that such increase of inflection as these poems attempt to objectify, would help toward such an accommodation.

I would like to thank William Everson for his steady encouragement, and for writing the foreword to this book. I would also like to thank Robert Duncan for his many suggestions.

Most of all: I am grateful to May for her loving guidance, and Karuna and Kiruba for all of their help. And especially: my friend and brother, Mr. A. M. Barnabass: to him this book is dedicated with love and gratitude.

W.R.

for BARNABASS

love is endless . . .

I : Dawn before the Storm Came

Owls
Les Trois Frères
13–11,000 B.C.

Madras: A Blind Child Dances with an Owl-Mask On

The child pounds on the drums,
and the crickets in the vault start.
The storm comes,
and the spiders in the ferns fall. Rain
hammers on the vaulted court;
and the humming of the creek bed
burns in the ghost-aisled field. Mist
floats on the creek like a feathered shield.
Clouds settle in the east;
from thicket to thicket: drummed
    in the tangle of the linnet's
stammering: coiled in the airborne yard;
scattered from the hoisted thicket
    of the blind child's voice. Crowds
huddled on the riverbank
turn to the pebbled ford,
drawn by the cult of a flute
    to the crowded shack. Garbed
in the shadows of the thorn's claws;
ruled by the distant cricket in the drumming
    of the storm's walls;
schooled by the shield of the roost;
drawn down by the clouded mask of the moon;
drawn down by the peril of a blind fall, the child
calls to the dawn: each gauze
disk of the dawn, each tower of the blinded dawn
    in the shutters of the owl's eyes: each
held-back, heart-beat hollow
    of the hooded echoing: dim as the distant
pummel of the ruined wheel
        in the locked chutes of the grainary.

And the child
dances out when the flute's notes start.
The purl of the owl's claws,
treading on the soaked stacks, falls.
And the webbed dawn of the dance starts.
Look! The joy of the child is shadowless:
the beaked voice drums in the dome of the rounded
sighted speech,
drawn to the doubled
fists of the blind child's hands. Each
held bloom, that the dawn brings, shines. Each
   flooded chord in the mute
halt of a cricket (*jewel* in a trod shell)
shines, gathered from the dawn's walls;
drawn from the infinite, poured
beauty of God. It is all there still.
                 And the child
sings: clear as the dart of a finch
   in the moon-carved cold, clear as the chipped,
masked power of the sunken garden (gathered
   by the chalked star in the depth of the song's blooms)
burns in the sound of its rise, rests
   in the sound of its fall:
calm as the outward-ordering
arch of a garden fountain:
fierce
   as the form of the fern's
small scroll: the infallible quill.

Mother's Chant for Her Child, Cremation Field, Madras

I burned my child
to a brown fall in a field.
Smoke rose
from the cleared stair
  in a tower of pain,
clung to the walled crowd
   in a barbed coil,
chilled by a thin
sweep, stormed
  into steep air, there,
where the heaped shroud
   of the mirrored field
fell, I turned, tearful;
came down
  the stone stairs.

I called a serpent chant to dance to: *dead*
the god-tongue of the wing-carved cold: calm
the guttered child of the charred shield
  of the blurred, robed gold:
drum of the towered sorrow: singe
   of the bird-white hands:
     drum of the heart,
   tilt of the garland-dancer: dim
the dawn, the burned yard told,   cold
dead, the dawn the burned yard told . . .

Drum-Chant of the Devil-Worshippers:
Moore Market, Madras

Report from a Madrasi witness:
"I saw the black-magicman stab the child to death, at least the blood
certainly looked real. Then they placed a towel over the body. When
they lifted it up, the child was gone. A few minutes later, the same child
came out from the crowd, laughing and dancing to the drum, as if
nothing had happened."

We have roamed
    in the walls of the hand's
detached twist; dwelt
in the shell of the heart:
the interior, crystalline pain:
groped the terrible spell
that aerial fear can do.
We are you, child, you.

There is no other love
when the thrown stars fall.
Set in the soul, we feel
the sudden
    groundless sadness: *wheel*
of the domed gold, gone.

In the shatter of foil,
in the fall of a shell,
we suck the yolk
    of a demon-child, spilled;
speak the shock of the howl
        that held him there:
It was light-years long;
    it was caught tight:
coiled shield of darkness,
demon-double of darkness:
mirror of the golden garden,
litter of light:
mirror of the infinite slaughter
    of sluice-draped sleep.

We were there, steep
    in the dome of the shadowless hood,
where the hushed crowd grieved,
we summoned the dark beak back.
But the charlatan rites of the dead
shall flood him down,
    shall shatter his light
out.
        Far out of sight
    in the pulse of the coiled sun,
            one in the shock of hate,
shall, round him, come
and drown him, shaded in sleep:
shall, far down the mute air,
cloud-bury him, deep,
where the hush of a thousand fallen
shudder the unbound fall.
And the drum
    stuns halls with its dark wings.

We have roamed
    in the walls of the hand's
detached twist; dwelt
in the shell of the heart;
the interior, crystalling pain;
        and the blood;
and the endless
            blaze of tears
from an unborn room.

Tiruchi Leprosarium:
I Dream of a Spider with a Goat's Head

Shaken awake by the tower's bells . . .
  And the rising mist of the rain
clings to the bronze poles of the roof.
Out, on the cobbled terrace of the ward,
I hear the sounds of the crowds
    in the aisles of the bulldozed wall.
I wake as the child calls: drums at the stricken
center of the worn-down field:
    from garden to garden of the court's stalls
the cries of the hawkers by the stacked
piles of the lotuses: claimed by the world,
I walk from the gutter to the combed
tilt of the wall: *forest*
  of the egg-sac filth
shadowing the tipped   blaze of the spinners:
The actual world: the end of the miracle:
the root-webbed
shield of the heart in the linear
ruin of the rain. Lost
  in the gauze-scythe of the earth:
the cupboard of the shell's coils: *void*
  of the crowded-out litter of the yard: gaunt
thicket of the deepened sutures: the dashed-down
trunk of the strewn fern's fall:
carried by the trapped
echo in the corridor, the dropped gauze
falls: *these*
wounds: walls of the shadowless lost.

Jungle-Swamp at Kutcheri Falls

Each death of faith and deeper
pausing for relief,

like a furl from the threaded seed
in a phantom valley,

tips in a globe of speech
to fathom God again,

and the poem's bloom
in a fern-grown glade,

follows the gathered flight
    of a tipped spore's fall

and the endless breathing
hides in a quill of shade.

II : The Calling of the Storm

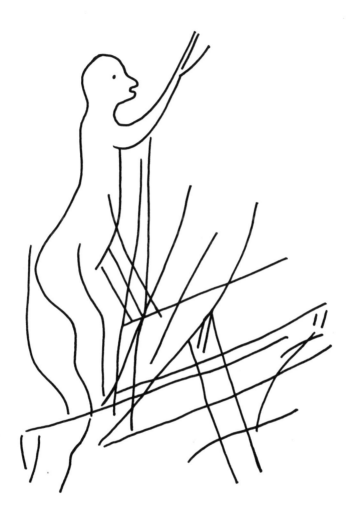

Monkey
Los Hornos
23–20,000 B.C.

Monkey-Devil Dance on Police Line Road

Moved down to the tense face:
moved like a cross to the trough of the chattering
sounding board of bloom:
turned, from trail to trail,
like a tipped bonnet in the air:
Fear stood in the loud field,
shunted to the gauze of the jarred thicket
to imitate the burial of the moon's
    sorrowing thorn;
strung, by the dreaded ruin
     scratched
  on the hooked beak of the butcherbird
chipped on the flawed shield: ribbed
  in the sudden sight of the serpent's
bouncing hood:
     clouted aside in the cuffed
gutter of the barbed floor: blurred
  by the flicker in the scrubbed
chorus of the child's voice: rocked in the terrible
chime-glide flight of the linnet's tongue's
stammering; from field to soaked field,
shunted into domed bloom:
There! by the skimmed stairs;
huddled at the locked door: cribbed
  in the sound of the loom
(in the sound of the linen hung in the lane)
drummed in the violent float of the moon-round yard:
    the Luminous Visitor.

Sea-Bird with a Broken Wing: Malarial Swamp at Adhyar

Sometimes
the dawn shall come
when the bird's eyes move
thousands of miles for water.

Sometimes
the dawn shall come
when the bird's eyes move
thousands of miles for water.

Ah, friend, friend,
after the storm falls;
after the tide comes with its own
mirrored shattering: the form of the serpent
cycles the serpent in: the bird
hides itself in the chalk-thicket of the dune.
The pillars of the wings, robed in their dark cloth, shake.

Sometimes the truth of the sand shows
what the storm's rise shows:
from star to tracked-down star, the terrible
cradle bestrewn with thorns.
Some thorns have mercy; the least source
shakes. And the netted garden falls.
    And the dreamt grass fades.
Drawn, by the lacquered chorus of the rain,
    in the mirrored aisle of the air,
over the moon, with its gauze-face,
    pure as a child's prayer:
drummed   by virtue of pity for pain
            in a steep-shaped fall, friend,
fear is the name for the fitted
stone we burn in sleep.

At an Altar Where Children
Were Sacrificed for Rain: Kangipuram

If the monsoon rain should fall:
if the world of a child falls,
these times shall come, Lord.
And the town shall weep
that suffers dryness now
where the first spring rose.

If the dome of the chalked ground
turns in the forest
   of the field-stone of Time,
do the crowds
form in the street?
Do they sometimes
  begin to explain
where the tiniest child
goes, when the dawn comes,
and the town's dogs moan?

When the throngs of the dancers
fade, when the broken
arm of the bent fern
falls,
     do they then speak,
as father, to daughter, does,
when the green bank burns,
and the mirror's eyes open?

When the chorus of the flute
fades,
when the burial of the cricket
sings,
     God knows:
They hear it in a trance of light
as the spirit of a dancer does:
unbearable: the devils' bells!

And the crowds
speak of the sun.
And the roots need rain.

But the heart needs
    innocence, oh,
like a dug spring!

Children's Ward of the Tiruchi Leper Colony
Armless Child Cries to Be Picked Up

I suppose most stones
are easier to move than these.
    God knows, the world has
limbs of years: shadows of rooms
with their own arms to raise.
This child has none. The relief,
that a hand feels from a clenched stone,
shines, falters and fades. Cries
    of the tended garden
wake in the ward: tide of the sword
    of the sea: more and more of the truth
that was most loved, lost. Who
knows what seed from the yard, what
shell-jewel in the will
enters the room, from the haze-wound
    of the world: the star-
stillness of space, speaks,
    from the burial wall of the garden's
endless mending-room of prayer?
I know that deep cry:
    towering out to the stacked
drums of the reef:
as a thorn keeps pace with a rose;
as a bell burns back
        from the rounded
dark of the ward, I reach
    to the dimmed-down
shuffle of the child's
raised fist. It is
fading away:
    as the touched
form of the tiniest
held child sways. Yes,
I am calm, yes, I am
calm, now: I am
    ruined.

The Rise of the Serpent, the Doom of the Sighted Fawn

According to local Madras report, a woman, in possession of black market
gold, desperate to get past the dock guards at the harbor, dazed by a devil-
promise she had once made for money, killed her own child, and filled his
body with the stolen gold. She was discovered when a guard, who was
checking her, noticed the slump of the child's head.

She told the guard about the loom's
least lace. Turned
to see the tipped stone fall. She
spoke of a perfectly reasoned
field of light, as the shocked
voice of a blind child might. But
the form of her face ceased, as if some fawn
        had started out
from heart-beat to heart-beat: *trot*
  of aerial wall, swell of a leaf,
clumped in shaded field, fern and thorn.
And hidden then. *How can I shield you, child?*
Grief blooms: here, there: travelling over
the black dock, shunted down to doom.
    She called a storm to come:
the prize rose ruled,
battling loud air to a sheer fall.
She called down, alone, a dawn:
  a dome-shaped field, child: fawn.
Infinite, the blurred load
snagged.
    The hooded rattling
struck back in a gauze-rose rush.

III : When the Lightning Fell

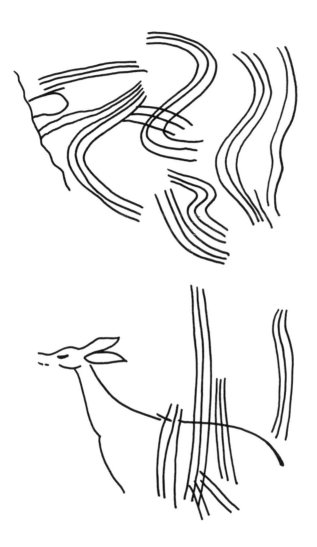

Fawn
Altamira
17–13,000 B.C.

At the Bed of a Child Dying of Cholera

For him, in the noon heat:
fever, the fire-sword of pain.
The child, stored in dawn-gold,
gathers to rust. The rust
roots doom in the seen thing: the picture
   over the bed:
the spring of a galloping,
     desolate, bold,
mirrored garden of brown:
fawn of a mule deer, blurred
   in the shaken thicket:
throat, caught, in the midst of a globed bound.
And the sword of the sun shines.
I hear it; bear it, lonely. The room
endures slowness. Your mother falls.
     The doom, that bore you, weeps.
Could only the storm be *done*
with the hurl of the tiger's eyes
that overarches the air; the fever
burn it to be, that enters thunder shadowless,
falls, in the least mist; yes, even the rain . . .
Could only the tiger weep for the fawn's fall,
then could we bear it, child;
nor, hearing him doing it, bleat
for the fall of the fawn, alone; your
mother carry us lost; and even the pain
would not have slowness, child,
   nor the least
live thing spilled.

Ah, but the heart, the heart:
the wing-sped, sorrowing seed;
and the white hot heat,
   come summer and summer,
even over the softest air: the guided spring.

And the fawn-doom grieves;
gathers all souls the same.
In the room of the tongue's slowed seed:
even the tinest
pod of the puff-ball
nods,
    and the sockets shatter.
And your mother knows what the sound brings
   of the worst fall: all, in an instant,
ended. Oh,
what a tall, what a towering, lightning
song befalls the hill:
one tiny, galloping twist
       of the dashed-down fawn,
and the ground sings.

For Devadas,
Decapitated by Shrapnel during a Parachute Jump

Nothing flies
that dies, then,
falls.

Except for Devadas
who died, then,
shining.

And something bright
that shone, then,
fell.
    He came across
a cloud-strewn spring.

And then,
    the doom
fell, the tipped shade
    mourned.
        Oh,

he danced the dance the blurred stones speak.

Remote, blurred, shadowless: the sound
  of a far star's sea . . .
              and it builds to an untold,
waving, gesturing risk of an infinite
span of prayer:
halts in th entering arch of the world:
the enthroned cloud's fall: each strict flight,
fanned into pure air by the flourish of the wind's notes
when it heaps dried sand by gathering seed; pushed
  from the hum of a hillside stir,
full-tilt to the sun:
  in the deep, slant
surge of underground green. And it comes into upturned bloom
    in the god-unfolding flight of all that is told in air:
each hill of color, there:
the hesitance of air,
when the spirit of a thousand swords, that allows streams,
falls. It summons the march, the voice, the shield to the blurred,
globed door—
the smashed bolt, the mirror: the terrible
echoing air: in the clouded blood of the room, in the round
foam of the seed; in the room-made-double, the howl:
the devil of darkness, cribbed, in the fear of the child;
stored in the darkened shield of the mountain:
higher than that, to a star-sized fall:
even higher: the fire, the dance of the anger of air,
when the heart, when the tilt of the heart—the bejeweled field
bound down in the bog's bones,
halts
  in a mirror of prayer,
in the ancient kindness of air; the approached speech—
the dealt syllable—
drums in the throats of the skimmed stars, speaks;
blooms as the dance of the world does, bright!
  in the thousand-sided sound of reflected flight:

in the held pearl's flash, yes, and it rings,
clear as the soul of a bell does: *loud,* domed to a *blast:* each
surface of battling air,
    drummed
  in the infinite lightning measureless fire of the *sheer air's*
clearest station of mirrored, aerial grace and dearest
        surface of God's
      face in the air: the heart
      the held child
       sings.

Nest of a Lotus Spider by a Cow Tank:
Tiruchi Leper Colony

The pail at the front of the cow tank falls.
Because of the force of the noon sun's heat,
my mind dims endlessly, and draws toward sleep.
I watch the parade of the dragging children
come to a hesitant standstill of stone.
They begin the hymn to the Lord God Rahm.
I cannot hear the choir of the carpeted voices:
    slump
  of the salt-asylum, drummed
from court to court of the faltering
storm-fire stair: the fluted tapping of endless
air that descends into sheer fire: star-spire:
spool of the blood thread:
               moss, shorn to the ground:
stump of the lichen, broken:
chalk of the ruined gauze in the gutter's
tracked float, skimmed: *shuffling*
  of the solitary quarter
    of the red-crab's
      perch: forest of the threaded-out
garden of the spiked trellis
  of the jarred-aside stone . . .

The pail at the front of the cow tank falls.

Morning Drum-Chant: In the Hill-Forest of Keethi

As the dawn comes; as the last stars fade:
this is the Truth, in the heart
    with its domed fall: each
fountain stored in the whole halt of the hill.
We are shaken awake by images, child,
as the form of the fawn shines:
from cloud, from thicket, from field,
drawn to the gathered edge of the orchard,
        only. only in air; the abrupt halt of the will:
the detached, spilled shield
            in the quicksilver sight of the sun:
like a globed dance it is done: when the lurch
    in the hesitant sprawl that allows speed fades:
            drawn down by the offered prayers of the drums;
        each
centered sound of the footfall formed by the thin feet,
            in the raised mist of the air. It is all
One: what the heart wants most, child, when the Host
shines in the hand: the restored field,
drawn, to the uttermost edge of the air
in the tilt of the heart, in the fanned sheen of the air:
drummed in the dance of the heart: when the fawn-form fades
    (far out of sight in the sun, to be soaring into it)
Christ's face!
            And, even in heaven: *seen!*

IV : When the Blind Storm Came

Le Gabillou
15,000 B.C.

Poem after the Exorcism of a Child Born Blind

Pain, clouted aside, child,
and the dark deed, done. The town's dogs
prowl the flooded field
    to a lichen-darkened wall.
        Can you find home?
There is still pain.

        I cannot shield you, child,
from the cringe of a blind fall:
burial of the cricket's nest,
    where the lost face speaks.
Turned to stone by the touch
  of the chill trail, child,
whenever I reach, each
  bitterness
      falls like an infinite
rain storm down. Can you find home?

These arms are *yours,* child.
The truth the soul can feel
becomes itself to fall. In the webbed
force of the dimmed-down dawn:
      you might do it well,
child, you *might* do it *well:* a song of sheltering:
It speaks back the bright-robed rain.
We hear *pools*
  caught, then:
the tipped pools do it, child:
and even the garden-blinded
      linnet
might do it: And the least
flooded pity's faltering pain: stitched
round the bell of a curb, and the held
doom of the leper's
bumped, dark itch-demon of pain.

God knows, their eyes rose
when the blind storm came; *dim*
    as even the lit, trailed gauze shows
following wounds down, deeper than death,
when cholera's stiff hope
blooms and masters comforting,
        and the dead house weeps.
Child, the linnet weeps, you move toward stone.
Even the pocketed stone told of child love:
the rain rang rooves over your head.
If you found home, child,
if you found home: if you found a heart-halt
here: if the throat's roots
ring to the ultimate
        heart-root ache,
behold the truth of the real world, child,
imagine it: task
    of the measured truth of the pure
veiled field: in the depth of the heart:
for a world that is born blind:
braille of the held moan;
        of the bent grief.

Spiral of Solitude, Denizen of Grief

From a story in a Bombay newspaper: While dining at a hotel, a Bombay resident found a child's finger in his soup. Subsequent inquiries by the police revealed that the owner had a small room in the back of his hotel where several hundred children had already been kept and starved to death. Most of them had been kidnapped from a poor section of the city and sold to the owner.

The stone of the heart speaks
when the flock gains air:
combed, calm, clear in a globed plot.

When the hesitant tilt of the mastered circle
starts to sing,
it fills the heart
    to a white-starred spring.

And the form of the lone crane
turns and circles aground
    from the gathering slant of the shore-flock,
flutters and sings like a kildeer does,
drawn to the bank on the torn
shield of its wings.

        Oh, but the wilted heart of the crane's
greed is motionless:
throned in a pool for hours,
with the fierce head
hunched forward to feed.
        In the aim of the harsh air
    where the spirits of serpents speak,
I have seen the cocked head
tilt and the lone crane
stab toads in the thick
blades of the reeds. I have felt afraid.

The most powerful call of all birds
is the crane's:
its voice: a test to tower the speeding shadow.
If ever the crane should speak,
and the tilted dark of the domed slab fall,
there could be no holiness,
nor the least
breath of strength
to break back the beak from the heart's
stone.

For the stone and citadel of the human heart
is holiness,
like a world, mirrored
        in a terrible spiral, steep.
I have heard the measured chorus of the god-heart
weep:
throned in a world where the sword of the serpent
sings. But the dome of the crane's
crescent-voice is deeper:
slick-sided,
        sickle-sided:
scum-throat, and thorn-blind cold.

Tiruchi Leprosarium: The Male Ward

Dropped on the ridge poles of the eaves,
the tent of a spider sways.
I cover the last
pail from the pump, and the cow tank
burns.
            On the foil of the chalked surfaces,
the bronze shells of the
                hollowed-out water bugs
jump, and are sucked downward.
Threads of the reeds shine
        on the domes of the humped roots.
They are buried in the tins of the lotuses,
hauled from the stacked gutter of the court
to the male ward,
        where,

        because of the wounds,
        the limbs
        are raised
        for years
            over the darkened linen. Pain
          in the skimmed
        gauze of the eyes,
        glows, like a child's does:
        deep, by each
                rocked bed,
        and the doom: by far:
        the loneliest disaster:
        spider's charges,
        dropped
        again and again, if the calm comes;
        raised steep, if the web shakes:
            still does the soul fall. Stumps
        drawn even higher
                to halt it again.

And they close in.

Dance of a Deaf-Mute at a Fire-Walking Ceremony

The crowd stands in the road.
The surface of the road feels
like the stone wall of a well.
The sand on the dark bank
burns the children's feet
   like enamelled metal

From court to court of the yard
I hear the mute's dance:
   the shuffling of the trapped
echoes. Beat
  by held-back heart beat
the swords shine.
         When the mute
comes to a halt,
the chorus of the flutes starts.

    And the chant
  of the silent
crowd in unison
drums in the throats
  of the doomed stones,
speaks.

V : The Whirlwind's Fall

Bull
Le Gabillou
16–13,000 B.C.

Drums of a Devil Cult near a Treadmill Wall:
Paddy-Field at Tiruchi

As I was riding in a train past the field listening to the drums, I overheard one of the survivors of the Bengal hurricane tell his friend, "As we were piling the bodies to be burned, we found a drowned child still holding tight to a small, toy pinwheel."

As the roots of the dead palm
bloom when the palm falls . . .

As the bullocks
haul the stone; as the stone
drums the dried food clean . . .

As the muffled words of the heart bloom,
shield to jeweled shield:

God knows,
no further
burden of song, no
stronger tongue can tell

how the storm
comes,
and the wheel of the child sings.

Canticle for Rajan's Daughter

Rajan told me how, some years ago, his daughter had gone down to a sea-
side village to show her gold-embroidered marriage-dress to a friend. A
swirling monsoon wind had swept her from the sea-cliff to the reef. Rajan
and his brother had recovered the body with a fishing net.

Brought down
from that high field, Lord?
there *is* no heavier rain.

Even the chalked net of the heart
can become frayed, Lord, how
can there be prayer for it? Pain
has none, nor allows prayers,
ever: to *whom*
shall the calm come
   when the drawn-back net
     of the dragging garden
falls, and the scythed
dome of the storm
burns itself to the wall?

Grief, like a fire-sword of cold, Lord:
each hand of the garden
raw with the held stone's
naked radiance: sprawl of the mirrored
sand and center of the whirlwind's
sheer fall,
   whose form has here no wall; can stand
no such
vast loss
as comes now
to the bronze speech of the voice,
drawn to the burial veil of the world.

there can be no darker water of grief,
when the gulls' calls fade, Lord, it is all
mask of the stone,

scythe of the sand,
sound of the carpeted sea:
  grudge of the massive
    might of the known
fall of the sea. How can there be prayer for it?
Lord, it was not right
for the arms of the sand
to bear such faltering: caught
  in the sea-fern filth
    of the drummed tide's
faltering: brought from the ancient
chorus of the reef to the crowded yard. Lord, God,
Christ!
Each
time; as the years
fade: again and again:
(if the monsoon rain should fall):
I remember the thicket of the spider's colors,
Lord, there can be no gathering island
easier to move than the webbed
dance of the forest's
aerial fall: disk of the held, jarred face
  on the outstretched
terrace of the crab's floor:
    as the whole heart of the world
grieves in the rocked
litter of the jeweler's garden:
chorus of the gulls' cries
where the launched dance sways.

Lord,
this dance of the heart
  in the dance of the water is dead.
There can be no heavier mirror (it is done)
  (if the green stairs fade) than the thread
  of a rising spider's
stone-crowned hood.

Song of Those Drowned in the Bengal Hurricane Disaster

Raised over the stone's space
was a dark space: eyes
rose, like leaves, lost
    in a carried
forest of water: trees
foamed with sheer
fathoms to fall: veils
sang. The song
spanned seas.

Bending over the reef's face
was a dark face: fear,
drummed into deeper water,
without sound,
sand the song from afar: fields
loomed
    in absolute shade,
spread where the arctic
ice-runs stand,
    under the vast sea like a final mountain. Oh,
we are nearly a million dead. We stand
        on the bed of the sea.
There was never a land of burial
robed in grief as ours was.

Nor hands to move
this huge, unbroken stone.

Prism for the Craft of Speech

When the forms
   of the prayers
fall,

they are colored blue.
As, on earth,
an animal: green;

or a glass fish.

VI : "Like a Blind Rain . . ."

Women & Child
Cogul
10,000 B.C.

Poem Sequence:

Possessed Nurse at the Maternity Ward of
The Child Jesus Hospital

From the Madras Government Museum Bulletin, Vol. LI, pg. 65:

At the Sessions Court, February ... five persons were charged with the murder of a young woman named Marayee. The theory put forward by the prosecution was that two of the accused practised sorcery, and were under the delusion that, if they could obtain possession of a foetus from the uterus of a woman, who was carrying her first child, they would be able to work some wonderful spells with its aid. With this object they entered into conspiracy with three other accused to murder a young married woman, aged about 17, who was 7 months advanced in pregnancy, and brutally murdered her, cutting open the uterus and removing the foetus contained therein. . . . Evidence was produced to prove that two of the accused decamped after the murder with a suspicious bundle, a few days before an eclipse of the moon, to Tricengode where there is a celebrated temple.

1. TOUR OF THE MATERNITY WARD
THE ROOM OF INTENSIVE CARE

To move
from this
one face,
mirrored
in its cringe
  of loss;
or see this fear,
like a clenched stone,
come to its own
deep shape in the dark:
God knows
there is no better mirror
than this hospital:
shrine
  of the unborn monkey
    in a glass
      crib.

Down in the yard of the ward
one solitary,
mange dog,
tethered by a corded chain,
snuffles at the domed door:
death
  is the dark
inheritance, moon
  of the trailed
shrine of the dead god's face; breath
of the hesitant body's
unbound fall; Oh,
ever I speak, Lord,
reach to the loss of the voice:
    the visitation of air:
call to the building stars, there;
even the standing gardens of the sea.
And in each
broken place
where the child falls,
can there be
    no human face, again, forever?

"Doom, then: doom:
and the doom be done."
      she said, then,
"Sir, and thy only
daughter be dead. And *these.*
These be thy brother's children: paws
    of the soured hands,
drummed on the stationed thorn; hooked
    from the backs of lanes. Ah,
down, down; let the round
    of the demon-darkness
shake him awake: let the cross
of the grave sea dissolve him,
thorn by thorn, in the air;
        taken from blind sleep
    to the death-enchanted
throne of the moon-god Rahm: there
where the sacred monkey
    (buried in the same wall, *twice: at the same time*)
rises.

And the stones rise.
And the mange dogs moan."

Whose death
to be brought down, Lord,
which is all ours? For *whom*
is the broken drum
of the blind word told,
    when the love that is soon said
falls into domed sound, speaks, thus, to kill:
and fills all the sad ward
    with the sores of Eden?
Oh, but hate comes fast, fast! It is sudden
IN.
If the hymns crack, the home
    of psalms is shaken.
Lord, God, Christ! I have seen,
    on the gauze of the strewn bed,
such tapping of eyeless hate
that descends into sheer fire: cliffed shroud
    on the domed tomb of the world!
And the hands of the child shake.
      Such faltering
stones do, when the doom comes
that frames a child in the wall.

Remembering the mirror, the rain:
    hearing
tapping at the domed door: sleep
builds stairs, stammering
too fast to trace.
      Who knows what
          face,
hunched, stored in the crib of Eden,
scattered from the worst fall: all
      tucked in,

comes to its own
deep shape in the dark. Ah,
and the nurse knows, raised as a child was, raised
as the massive oceans are,
from the peril of the trod sound
shrouded in the glass abyss: robed and knitted
      in the demon-garden: *she,* alone,
coming from the backs of lanes, knows
the bone-shattering shake of th cuffed twist,
        when the child falls
dead, when the doctor
staggers on the ruined stair;
peers, peers in the room: hammers
          on the domed door. Sleep
cowers in the mirror like a tense, stone hood. Sleep
forms itself in the mirror
    to the shape
        of an ape-like head.

6. AMPHITHEATER: THE OPERATION

As the shell of a pearl,
   to the moon, shows pain;
as the belled tide
bows to be ruled, nods
to be taken away,
she calls to the moon
and the jointed brightness carries him: thorns
float in the halt of the room as a dolphin does:
in the counted yard of the moon, fog, thorn,
         settling sea.
I have seen such flower and quarter of hate
     to split
the nerve's eyes open: cyst
   of the pure briar of air
where the soul's walls moan. I have seen this
     power of soundless darkness
breathe again. And she breathes again (And *does* she, then?)
   by the drawn-down
cower of the dog's delirium: death
snuffs life out. The pearl of the moon in the cringe
     of the aerial fountain
rages hours in the mask of the ice face.
It shows
    in the ruin of the water
what the stones ARE.

"Doom, then, doom;
and the doom be done,"
     she said, then,
"Sir, it is you. It has
not been born.
It needs your knives. Yes.
It needs your blessing."

God knows what the soul finds here.
Drummed from the ancient
terror that the hell's halls hold; FEAR.
The solemn ivory.
The monkey.
The self's
crushed face, everywhere: the hound, over it: Ah,

Who
has been born so lonely? The room
    is a demon litany. *Walls*
       imitate
    from glass to glass to glass:
the hoot, the chattering:
    the unborn head.

8. COUNTERSPELL FOR AN EXORCIST

When the doom comes, and the ape-dance starts,
Lord, if thou knowest falls,
save!

Drawn from the yard to the shrine of the wall
where the plumed stones speak:
Out from the moon to the quilted yard
    where the dark spokes, stored in the garden, fade:
over the cringe of the child's face, blest by a shaken star;
I climb to the vaulted room: even higher: the tower of flame: OH
GOD of the gods of gods: the alive floor
stoops to be dug into fire as a starved hound
digs, digs in a log, and the stored pain
grins and storms in the room like a blind rain . . .

Lord, turn tail that hell-hound here!
Lord! Lord! Fear
shaketh the will:
to have seen the hound that bayeth for the mind!

VII : The Aftermath

Man
Pech Merle
17–13,000 B.C.

Song-Cycle for Christ the Lord:
On a Child's Death by Diving

It happened, at a farm-pool in the region of Kaapadi, that the owner of the farm, being filled with anger because the children from a nearby workhouse used the pool for a diving place, staked it out with a series of sharpened pilings. That same night, the first of the fierce monsoon rains fell. The pool was flooded. The stakes could not be seen.

I.

The rain
falls. The choirs
of the town's bells
fade. No other
webbed burden of song
could do it
quite so well. Down
where the aisles
   of the orchards are,
drawn to the fluted
channel
of the road-tracked field,
held tight to the outspread
stance of a domed fall:
the child
is dead;
the blood, the child shed,
stone.

2.

Love has no
spirit of guilt
to shield a child from water:
No further pain
    on the jeweled tread of the floor;
no further
detached halt
    of the strewn field could tell
how far the guiltless
spilled form of the heart
had fallen down in fire;
dumped like a soaked bell
full-tilt to the sprawled stone:
held by the truth of its own
fitted weight to the blurred,
    chilled
reach of the blood-soaked stakes.
God knows I have gathered and held
each outstretched
thorn of the child's fall,
from the bronze field of the air
    to the jeweled floor.
Dear Lord, God, Christ,
do you hold him close? *I hold him close*
as the heart's dance does
when a child sings.

The Chant the Ooty Midwife Sang

Report from a Badaga villager: "We never go down to that grove at night. A long time ago, a group of monkeys carried off a child and killed her. Ever since then, that lower grove has been haunted. Many have heard her down there, crying out in the dark."

Prologue

Years, we have lived on this dark mountain. Death is a sad fall. The stone
becomes a field. *These* children fear the rain, now, in the tall,
stone trees. When I was twelve, I climbed them *all.* I would not come down.
I remember, yes. There were many more flocks
of green birds in the hills. The flood was over, a small,
cold wind came, a wide wind. A wind that turns leaves
for the soft sides to show, and awaits night . . .

The Chant

I remember the mute
net of the moon. The dawn
of the monsoon fell.
And the pitched flute
    of the dart bird sang.
I remember the hush in the creek
    of the cart path bend:
acres of water!

They came to take her away:
the daughter, the dancer of God,
    by the cliff of the steep, rock
doom that allows falls.
Her mother was blind.
She followed, from ledge to ledge,
    from stair to jeweled stair,
hands, caught by the bank of the threaded creepers.
But the hill storm struck.
and the thorn of the voice is lame.

And when I remember her mother, oh,
strewn clouds of her hair!
the loom of the infinite, gathering art
    of the god-mind there! But even the moon-stone
stitch of the voice is lame,
and the drum of the voice is lame; yes,
caught in the float of the heart, the *dome*
of the sweet song changed:
fluttering down the ledge like a strung bell . . .

Drummed like an infinite host from hell,
the howler monkeys of Ooty
fell, in numberless, banked glides to the hut:
carried off one of our tribe's untended children;
strung her with thin vines to the high trees . . .

They came to take her: the daughter of stormed air.
She has, from dome to dome of the soaring garden, gone;
down in the flute of the dart bird, gone; *rose*
when the fall of the hill storm struck
    and the God-mind moved, even in air,
        yes,
those
    who have, in darkness, been;
        yes,
those   who cling to the tall, stone trees; yes,
those who fell   in groundless darkness:
        have, in the grove of the green bird, been. Yes:
Those who know what shall be spoken: *pain,*
roam the rocks of the night in a blind rain . . .

The Gift of the Leper Child

Offered: the lotus
blooms like a held field
from all sides the same. It towers
    like a stationed angel,
robed in a stream of flame: down the dark
slope: the dealt
wars of the wings. Each
gathered edge of the flower is open: the flames, in the roots
  of the God-unfolding, rise. Arms
    of the shaded gold unfold in breathless focus:
the heart bursts into full bloom,
held in the endless, swept float of the air
like a proud child's prize
discovery of shell.
                  But the shell falls.
And the outstretched blaze of the child's stump:
it is (oh) the merest, least, lost,
cupped gathering of hands.

His face is the endless fall of a stone city.

I go down *here,* over the steep
bloom of the God-unfolding;
bend; bear deeper evil:
   spike, and burn, in the darkness, stalk and stone.

Shore Temple at Mahabalipuram

Note: The favorite animal of the god Murgan is a peacock. *Murgah solloo* means, in Tamil, "Answer us, O Murgan!" Murgan usually appears to his worshippers in the form of a small child of unearthly beauty.

Sing praise and glory alone,
roost of the cliffed stone,
bank of the burial isle of the world
   where the crushed stairs fade: *Murgah, solloo!*

In the chime-glide flower
   of the star-fish voice,
gathered and stashed tight
   in the banked sound of the sea: *Murgah, solloo!*

by the bronze gauze of the throne,
sing praise and glory alone
   at the foot of the dashed-down
flame
     when the throne falls,
        when the plumed grace of the heart
comes to its own
     fork-shaped fall: *Murgah, solloo!*

Solloo, Murgah, solloo! When the priceless crown
has fallen down in fire
stands, lost in the rain,
sing praise and glory to God,
as the scythed voice falls,
        as the death-temple of Murgan falls
like a beak-struck bell:
sing praise and glory to God,
whose love has guidance for us, yes,
as the dawn does, darkness;
or the moon, the sea.

VIII : Final Songs of Sheltering

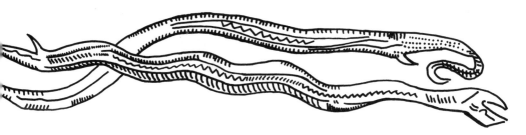

Snake
Montgaudier
12,000 B.C.

Sutra for Some Village Children, Struck by Famine: Mahabalipuram

Note: In Mahabalipuram there is a giant rock-carving depicting the sudden descent of the Ganges river during a famine. Divine love for the poor is thus the theme. Yet the portrayal of the river's power is more erotic than compassionate: several couples are staring, enchanted, at two strange forms in the water: forms, part human and part serpent-like.

The distant torrent
   of the jointed dancing
drums in the thicket of the thorn's spells.
Friend, if the stone's chorus
keeps the heart from the heart,
it is perilous, yes: the endless
troth of the god and the goddess
thus: apart. They did it
as a garland dancer does:
as a tipped stone torch does,
built by the constant torrent
   of the soul's fear
as it fountains after us; each
solitary halt at the throne
   of the hillside
     stone shrine, spilt.
Oh, that a waterfall-fashioned face,
veiled in the lust-brand of the wall,
should cast the shield of the mirror
sheer *mountainsides* down? Each
scaled stone of the poised domes
down? No pity for the dead?
No flute in the heart of the slaughtered thicket
that the reed bird built?
    No pity for the dead?
No pity for the (ah!) for the blinded
bone of the sunken faces: choir
   of the innocent
children's faces:
hands, raised; eyes, solemn with loss?

Thus: the peril of the domed bronze
falls. Thus
the solitary doom of the cliffed shattering:
from hut to hut, the terror of the wounded hood.
For the time was, friend,
when the ruined shield was gold
and the blood that the god shed: stone.
There, where the webbed
shadow of the moon stood, in its domed
pity for the blind:
Pain rose
in the dust-voice of the rock.
Pain danced in the first
sand of the world:
cupped, deep, in the heart,
where the spirits of children sing,
    by the pivot of the *tracked*
comet of the rain,
      when the ground of the star that is closest to us
answers us: each
travelling sword of the mirror that is broken open.
Now that tilt of the broad stone
drums into infinite act. *Pain*
is the oldest of the dancers of God.
In the forest of the lacquered drum,
it allowed streams. NOW
the pity, that the heart feels,
shines.

      Friend, we are drawn down
     in the tears of a blind fall.
See how *still*
the solemn children stand.
Oh, may the pain and the fear of it finish forever!

Up in the Bell Tower of the Temple for Child-Sacrifice at Taanjur; A Friend Tells of His Attempted Suicide

You cannot recall the unspent
form of the buried stone.
But friend, no child
who remained behind
could *ever* remember it,
death being, for all mankind,
what the sudden
growth of childhood meant
    by the turning-around of its own
carried stillness.

Now, in the sunken voice of the rain,
where the lifted children
fell, by the pounded
stone of the heart, we are chained blind;
friend, how bright, in the light of the dawn,
we are caught like a dancer's veiled fist:
drawn down to the padded
flood of the rain-soaked stairs:
brought up by the burial of the mirror to the rocked
dome of the temple's
feathered trellis of sleep.
Death comes like a cat's face in the eaves.
This
    is what your father meant
      by the garden of Eden: the dark
spokes of the roots: scattered in the walled pool:
plush of fern in the yard, bent
    like a sword in the orchard,
following the drag of the bald moon
      when the nine-day-buried demon
crawls, sick from the well: *guilt*
married to guilt: with the ground,
raised to the globed voice of a child:
      half-heard, from that depth,
downward: the undiminished,
scythed

sound of the town's bells,
stored by the mirrored tilt of the heart
in the pure air, forever.

Under the moon, the throngs of the muted chanters
bathe, bound, as the walls shine:
chalk of the brightness carries them: *blest,*
the upturned gauze of the palm
traces it out into light
 with the ground of the fairest
growth of its own
silence beyond praise.
  Oh, blythe
grace, drawn to the crest of the rain's
unfolding fiame; be not so certain to fall.
Call mother and father: the lit
fire in the wall: the cliffed
form of the heart: the only
bearable way: having come this far, by love,
this day: May the whole hate of the heart,
for the heart's sake, cease.

Scattered, from where we stand,
over the throngs in the yard, wishing them all well,
domed in the shadowless air, as it gathers all energy in:
God, knows, friend,
it is better, the fountain speak
 in the scope of its own fall:
better, by far, if these
dark, dismembered stones
knew God in the gold stones of their eyes:
death, being the rise of the weightless moon,
when the dear
mirror of it ends: the webbed
palm, with its trellis of roses,
falls: the stump
rots in the sun: crowds
ring
the bell
to call hearts
home.

For Barna

Beyond the birth of sighted stone
that built to a temple of prayer;

beyond the blinded gold of love
        that has no fame but spring;

    out of the heart of the gaunt
wounds of age: like a drummed cloud,
bent into total reverence,
        under the walls of the vast,
cliffed stone even steeper than death:
                        for you,
dear friend of God, I pray,
lost in the endless darkness
        of all things not yet loved:

I move to the shaded world of love,
like a small, blind
voice in the house
(singing).

Cobra at Floodtime; Govindamedu

Some may need years
to follow the brightness of this
crass loss that bends us over,
bird-close in the rain. Even the least
call to a child: it is old; it is (ah) it is
untold pain
Some may stand forever. Over the lost field
the river follows disaster.
And even the dead have tears, child, so many to fall:
nor comes ever the last.
Some stand like stationed trees,
as near doom to a fall as the wrist of a leaf: death
blooms, from all sides, blind.
It is fear, fear that bends us, child: we shiver
in a grim sleep; build
in a barbed void:
            drawn by the dawn to the least
lone fall;
and the pure fear of the self, sobbing to sight.

Poised to be sourced in speed, the cobra rises.
The birds' sounds fall.

        Love's voice vaults into the air,
      that holds us,
sings all fear down scythe
        through the sounding metal;
burns fields like a bell about to break.
And what such brightness *brings,* child: the whole air
shines back into one!

And love is old, child; and love is endless:
in a field—*in a pure field*—child,
where the darkness sends us,
when the day ends, child; when the domed voice
bends down over the other water forever.

Design: John McBride
Composition: Bill Rock
Printing: Braun-Brumfield
Distribution: SBD